The Baptist Catechism Journal

Locusts & Wild Honey Press

Q. 1. Who is the first and best of beings?

A. God is the first and best of beings. (Isaiah 44:6; Psalm 8:1; 97:9)

Q. 2. What is the chief end of man?
A. Man's chief end is to glorify God and to enjoy Him forever. (1 Cor. 10:31; Psalm 73:25-26)

Q. 3. How do we know there is a God?

A. The light of nature in man, and the works of God, plainly declare that there is a God; but His Word and Spirit only, do effectually reveal Him unto us for our salvation. (Rom. 1:18-20; Psalm 19:1,2; 2 Tim. 3:15; 1 Cor. 1:21-24; 1 Cor. 2:9,10)

Q. 4. What is the Word of God?
A. The Scriptures of the Old and New Testaments, being given by divine inspiration, are the Word of God, the only infallible rule of faith and practice. (2 Peter 1:21; 2 Timothy 3:16,17; Isaiah 8:20)

Q. 5. How do we know that the Bible is the Word of God?
A. The Bible evidences itself to be God's Word by the heavenliness of its doctrine, the unity of its parts, its power to convert sinners and to edify saints; but the Spirit of God only, bearing witness by and with the Scriptures in our hearts, is able fully to persuade us that the Bible is the Word of God. (1 Cor. 2:6,7,13; Ps. 119:18, 129; Acts 10:43, 26:22; Acts 18:28; Heb 4:12; Ps. 19:7-9; Rom. 15:4; John 16:13,14; 1 John 2:20-27; 2 Cor. 3:14-17)

Q. 6. May all men make use of the Scriptures?
A. All men are not only permitted, but commanded and exhorted, to read, hear, and understand the Scriptures. (John 5:39; Luke 16:29; Acts 8:28-30; 17:11)

Q. 7. What do the Scriptures principally teach?
A. The Scriptures principally teach what man is to believe concerning God and what duty God requires of man. (2 Tim. 3:16,17; John 20:31; Acts 24:14; 1 Cor. 10:11; Eccles. 12:13)

Q. 8. What is God?

A. God is a Spirit, infinite, eternal, and unchangeable in His being, wisdom, power, holiness, justice, goodness and truth. (John 4:24; Ps. 147:5; Ps. 90:2; James 1:17; Rev. 4:8; Ps. 89:14; Exod. 34:6,7; 1 Tim. 1:17)

Q. 9. Are there more gods than one?
A. There is but one only, the living and true God. (Deut. 6:4; Jeremiah 10:10)

Q. 10. How many persons are there in the Godhead?
A. There are three persons in the Godhead, the Father, the Son, and the Holy Spirit; and these three are one God, the same in essence, equal in power and glory. (1 Cor. 8:6; John 10:30; John 14:9; Acts 5:3,4; Matt. 28:19; 2 Cor. 13:14)

Q. 11. What are the decrees of God?
A. The decrees of God are His eternal purpose, according to the counsel of His will, whereby for His own glory, He has fore-ordained whatsoever comes to pass (Eph. 1:11; Rom. 11:36; Dan. 4:35)

Q. 12. How does God execute His decrees?
A. God executes His decrees in the works of creation and providence.
(Gen. 1:1; Rev. 4:11; Matt. 6:26; Acts 14:17)

Q. 13. What is the work of creation?
A. The work of creation is God's making all things of nothing, by the Word of His power, in the space of six days, and all very good. (Gen. 1:1; Heb. 11:3; Ex. 20:11; Gen. 1:31)

Q. 14. How did God create man?
A. God created man male and female, after His own image, in knowledge, righteousness, and holiness, with dominion over the creatures. (Gen. 1:27; Col. 3:10; Eph. 4:24; Gen. 1:28)

Q. 15. What are God's works of providence?
A. God's works of providence are His most holy, wise, and powerful preserving and governing all His creatures, and all their actions. (Neh. 9:6; Col. 1:17; Heb. 1:3; Ps. 103:19; Matt. 10:29,30)

Q. 16. What special act of providence did God exercise towards man, in the estate wherein he was created?
A. When God had created man, He entered into a covenant of works with him, upon condition of perfect obedience, forbidding him to eat of the tree of the knowledge of good and evil, upon pain of death. (Gen. 2:16,17; Gal. 3:12; Rom. 5:12)

Q. 17. Did our first parents continue in the estate wherein they were created?

A. Our first parents, being left to the freedom of their own will, fell from the estate wherein they were created, by sinning against God. (Gen. 3:6; Eccles. 7:29; Rom. 5:12)

Q. 18. What is sin?
A. Sin is any want of conformity unto, or transgression of, the law of God. (1 John 3:4; Rom. 5:13)

Q. 19. What was the sin whereby our first parents fell from the estate wherein they were created?
A. The sin whereby our first parents fell from the estate wherein they were created, was their eating the forbidden fruit. (Gen. 3:6,12,13)

Q. 20. Did all mankind fall in Adam's first transgression?
A. The covenant being made with Adam, not only for himself but for his posterity, all mankind, descending from him by ordinary generation, sinned in him, and fell with him in his first transgression. (1 Cor. 15:21,22; Rom. 5:12,18,19)

Q. 21. Into what estate did the fall bring mankind?
A. The fall brought mankind into an estate of sin and misery. (Ps. 51:5; Rom. 5:18,19: Is. 64:6)

Q. 22. Wherein consists the sinfulness of that estate whereunto man fell?
A. The sinfulness of that estate whereunto man fell, consists in the guilt of Adam's first sin, the want of original righteousness, and the corruption of his whole nature, which is commonly called original sin, together with all actual transgressions which proceed from it. (Rom. 5:19; 3:10; Eph. 2:1; Is. 53:6; Ps. 51:5; Matt. 15:19)

Q. 23. What is the misery of that estate whereunto man fell?
A. All mankind, by their fall lost communion with God, are under His wrath and curse, and so made liable to all the miseries of this life, to death itself, and to the pains of hell forever. (Gen. 3:8,24; Eph. 2:3; Gal. 3:10; Rom. 6:23; Matt. 25:41-46; Ps. 9:17)

Q. 24. Did God leave all mankind to perish in the estate of sin and misery?

A. God, out of His mere good pleasure, from all eternity, having chosen a people to everlasting life, did enter into a covenant of grace, to deliver them out of the estate of sin and misery, and to bring them into an estate of salvation, by a Redeemer. (Eph. 1:3,4; 2 Thess. 2:13; Rom. 5:21; Acts 13:48; Jer. 31:33)

Q. 25. Who is the Redeemer of God's elect?
A. The only Redeemer of God's elect is the Lord Jesus Christ, who, being the eternal Son of God, became man, and so was and continues to be God and man, in two distinct natures and one person, forever. (Gal. 3:13;1 Tim. 2:5; John 1:14; 1 Tim. 3:16; Rom. 9:5; Col. 2:9)

Q. 26. How did Christ, being the Son of God, become man?
A. Christ, the Son of God became man by taking to himself a true body and a reasonable soul; being conceived by the power of the Holy Spirit in the womb of the Virgin Mary and born of her, yet without sin. (Heb. 2:14; Matt. 26:38; Luke 2:52; John 12:27; Luke 1:31,35; Heb. 4:15; 7:26)

Q. 27. What offices does Christ execute as our Redeemer?
A. Christ, as our Redeemer, executes the offices of a prophet, of a priest, and of a king, both in His estate of humiliation and exaltation. (Acts 3:22; Heb. 5:6; Ps. 2:6)

Q. 28. How does Christ execute the office of a prophet?
A. Christ executes the office of a prophet, in revealing to us, by this Word and Spirit, the will of God for our salvation. (John 1:18; 14:26; 15:15)

Q. 29. How does Christ execute the office of a priest?
A. Christ executes the office of a priest, in His once offering up of Himself, a sacrifice to satisfy divine justice, and reconcile us to God, and in making continual intercession for us. (1 Peter 2:24; Heb. 9:28; Eph. 5:2; Heb. 2:17; 7:25; Rom. 8:34)

Q. 30. How does Christ execute the office of a king?
A. Christ executes the office of a king, in subduing us to Himself, in ruling and defending us, and in restraining and conquering all His and our enemies. (Ps. 110:3; Matt. 2:6; 1 Cor. 15:25)

Q. 31. Wherein did Christ's humiliation consist?
A. Christ's humiliation consisted in His being born, and that in a low condition, made under the law, undergoing the miseries of this life, the wrath of God, and the cursed death of the cross, in being buried, and continuing under the power of death for a time. (Luke 2:7; Gal. 4:4; Is. 53:3; Luke 22:44; Matt. 27:46; Phil. 2:8; Matt. 12:40; Mark 15:45,46)

Q. 32. Wherein consists Christ's exaltation?
A. Christ's exaltation consists in His rising again from the dead on the third day, in ascending up into heaven, in sitting at the right hand of God the Father, and in coming to judge the world at the last day. (1 Cor. 15:4; Acts 1:11; Mark 16:19; Acts 17:31)

Q. 33. How are we made partakers of the redemption purchased by Christ?

A. We are made partakers of the redemption purchased by Christ, by the effectual application of it to us, by His Holy Spirit. (John 3:5,6; Titus 3:5,6)

Q. 34. How does the Spirit apply to us the redemption purchased by Christ?
A. The Spirit applies to us the redemption purchased by Christ, by working faith in us, and thereby uniting us to Christ in our effectual calling. (Eph. 2:8; 3:17)

Q. 35. What is effectual calling?
A. Effectual calling is the work of God's Spirit, whereby, convincing us of our sin and misery, enlightening our minds in the knowledge of Christ, and renewing our wills, He does persuade and enable us to embrace Jesus Christ, freely offered to us in the Gospel. (2 Tim. 1:9; John 16:8-11; Acts 2:37; 26:18; Ezekiel 36:26; John 6:44,45; 1 Cor. 12:3)

Q. 36. What benefits do they that are effectually called, partake of in this life?

A. They that are effectually called, do in this life partake of justification, adoption, sanctification, and the several benefits which in this life do either accompany or flow from them. (Rom. 8:30; Gal. 3:26; 1 Cor. 6:11; Rom. 8:31,32; Eph. 1:5; 1 Cor. 1:30)

Q. 37. What is justification?
A. Justification is an act of God's free grace, wherein He pardons all our sins, and accepts us as righteous in His sight, only for the righteousness of Christ imputed to us, and received by faith alone. (Rom. 3:24; Eph. 1:7; 2 Cor. 5:21; Rom. 5:19; Phil. 3:9; Gal. 2:16)

Q. 38. What is adoption?
A. Adoption is an act of God's free grace, whereby we are received into the number, and have a right to all the privileges of the sons of God. (1 John 3:1; John 1:12; Rom. 8:16,17)

Q. 39. What is sanctification?
A. Sanctification is a work of God's free grace whereby we are renewed in the whole man after the image of God, and are enabled more and more to die unto sin, and live unto righteousness. (2 Thess. 2:13; Eph. 4:23,24; Rom. 6:11)

Q. 40. What are the benefits which in this life do accompany or flow from justification, adoption, and sanctification?
A. The benefits which in this life do accompany or flow from justification, adoption, and sanctification, are, assurance of God's love, peace of conscience, joy in the Holy Spirit, increase of grace, and perseverance therein to the end. (Rom. 5:1-5; 14:17; Prov. 4:18; 1 Peter 1:5;1 John 5:13)

Q. 41. What benefits do believers receive from Christ at death?
A. The souls of believers are at death made perfect in holiness, and do immediately pass into glory, and their bodies, being still united to Christ, do rest in their graves till the resurrection. (Heb. 12:23; Phil. 1:23; 2 Cor. 5:8; Luke 23:43; 1 Thess 4:14; Is. 57:2; Job 19:26)

Q. 42. What benefits do believers receive from Christ at the Resurrection?

A. At the resurrection, believers become raised up in glory, shall be openly acknowledged and acquitted in the day of judgment, and made perfectly blessed in the full enjoyment of God to all eternity. (Phil. 3:20,21; 1 Cor. 15:42,43; Matt. 10:32; 1 John 3:2; 1 Thess. 4:17)

Q. 43. What shall be done to the wicked at death?
A. The souls of the wicked shall at death, be cast into the torments of hell, and their bodies lie in their graves till the resurrection and judgement of the great day. (Luke 16:22-24; Ps. 49:14)

Q. 44. What shall be done to the wicked at the day of judgement?
A. At the day of judgement, the bodies of the wicked, being raised out of their graves, shall be sentenced, together with their souls, to unspeakable torments with the devil and his angels forever. (Dan. 12:2; John 5:28,29; 2 Thess. 1:9; Matt. 25:41)

Q. 45. What is the duty which God requires of man?
A. The duty which God requires of man, is obedience to His revealed will. (Micah 6:8; Eccles. 12:13; Ps. 119:4; Luke 10:26-28)

Q. 46. What did God at first reveal to man for the rule of his obedience?
A. The rule which God at first revealed to man for his obedience was the moral law. (Rom. 2:14,15; 5:13,14)

Q. 47. Where is the moral law summarily comprehended?
A. The moral law is summarily comprehended in the Ten
Commandments. (Deut. 10:4; Matt. 19:17)

Q. 48. What is the sum of the Ten Commandments?
A. The sum of the Ten Commandments is, to love the Lord our God, with all our heart, with all our soul, with all our strength, and with all our mind; and our neighbor as ourselves. (Matt. 22:36-40; Mark 12:28-33)

Q. 49. What is the preface to the Ten Commandments?
A. The preface to the Ten Commandments is, "I am the Lord thy God, which have brought thee out of the land of Egypt, out of the house of bondage." (Exodus 20:2)

Q. 50. What does the preface to the Ten Commandments teach us?
A. The preface to the Ten Commandments teaches us, that because God is the Lord, and our God and Redeemer, therefore we are bound to keep all His commandments. (Deut 11:1)

Q. 51. Which is the first commandment?
A. The first commandment is, "Thou shalt have no other Gods before me." (Exodus 20:3)

Q. 52. What is required in the first commandment?
A. The first commandment requires us to know and acknowledge God to be the only true God, and our God, and to worship and glorify Him accordingly. (Joshua 24:15; 1 Chron. 28:9; Deut. 26:17; Ps. 29:2; Matt. 4:10)

Q. 53. What is forbidden in the first commandment?
A. The first commandment forbids the denying, or not worshipping and glorifying the true God, as God and our God; and the giving that worship and glory to any other, which is due unto Him alone. (Joshua 24:27; Rom. 1:20,21; Ps. 14:1; Rom. 1:25)

Q. 54. What are we especially taught by these words, "before me," in the first commandment?

A. These words, "before me", in the first commandment, teach us, that God, who sees all things, takes notice of, and is much displeased with the sin of having any other God. (Deut.30:17,18; Ps. 44:20,21; Ps. 90:8)

Q. 55. Which is the second commandment?

A. The second commandment is, "Thou shalt not make unto thee any graven image, or any likeness of any thing that is in heaven above, or that is in the earth beneath, or that is in the water under the earth. Thou shalt not bow down thyself to them, nor serve them; for I the Lord thy God am a jealous God, visiting the iniquity of the fathers upon the children, unto the third and fourth generation of them that hate me: and showing mercy unto thousands of them that love me and keep my commandments." (Exodus 20:4-6)

Q. 56. What is required in the second commandment?
A. The second commandment requires the receiving, observing, and keeping pure and entire, all such religious worship and ordinances, as God has appointed in His Word. (Deut. 32:46; Matt. 28:20; Deut. 12:32)

Q. 57. What is forbidden in the second commandment?
A. The second commandment forbids the worshipping of God by images, or any other way not appointed in His Word. (Rom. 1:22,23; Deut. 4:15,16; Matt. 15:9; Col. 2:18)

Q. 58. What are the reasons annexed to the second commandment?
A. The reasons annexed to the second commandment, are, God's sovereignty over us, His propriety in us, and the zeal He has for His own worship. (Ps. 45:11; Ex. 34:14; 1 Cor. 10:22)

Q. 59. Which is the third commandment?
A. The third commandment is, "Thou shalt not take the name of the Lord thy God in vain: for the Lord will not hold him guiltless that taketh his name in vain." (Exodus 20:7)

Q. 60. What is required in the third commandment?
A. The third commandment requires the holy and reverent use of God's names, titles, attributes, ordinances, words, and works. (Ps.29:2; Deut. 32:1-4; Deut.28:58,59; Ps.111:9; Matt. 6:9, Eccles. 5:1; Ps. 138:2, Job 36:24; Rev. 15:3,4; Reve 4:8)

Q. 61. What is forbidden in the third commandment?
A. The third commandment forbids all profaning and abusing of any thing whereby God makes Himself known. (Malachi 1:6,7; Lev. 20:3;19:12; Matt. 5:34-37; Isa. 52:5)

Q. 62. What is the reason annexed to the third commandment?
A. The reason annexed to the third commandment is, that howsoever the breakers of this commandment may escape punishment from men, yet the Lord our God will not suffer them to escape His righteous judgment. (Deut. 28:58,59; Malachi 2:2)

Q. 63. Which is the fourth commandment?
A. The fourth commandment is, "Remember the Sabbath day to keep it holy. Six days shalt thou labor and do all thy work; but the seventh day is the Sabbath of the Lord thy God: in it thou shalt not do any work, thou, nor thy son, nor thy daughter, thy manservant, nor thy maid servant, nor thy cattle, nor thy stranger that is within thy gates: for in six days the Lord made heaven and earth, the sea, and all that in them is, and rested the seventh day: wherefore the Lord blessed the Sabbath day and hallowed it." (Exodus 20:8-11)

Q. 64. What is required in the fourth commandment?
A. The fourth commandment requires the keeping holy to God such set times as He has appointed in His Word, expressly one whole day in seven to be a holy Sabbath to Himself. (Lev. 19:30; Deut. 5:12)

Q. 65. Which day of the seven has God appointed to be the weekly Sabbath?

A. From the creation of the world to the resurrection of Christ, God appointed the seventh day of the week to be the weekly Sabbath; and the first day of the week ever since, to continue to the end of the world, which is the Christian Sabbath. (Gen. 2:3; John 20:19; Acts 20:7; 1 Cor. 16:1,2; Rev. 1:10)

Q. 66. How is the Sabbath to be sanctified?
A. The Sabbath is to sanctified by a holy resting all that day, even from such worldly employments and recreations as are lawful on other days, and spending the time in the public and private exercises of God's worship, except so much as is to be taken up in the works of necessity and mercy. (Lev. 23:3; Isa. 58:13,14; Isa. 66:23; Matt. 12:11,12)

Q. 67. What is forbidden in the fourth commandment?
A. The fourth commandment forbids the ommission or careless performance of the duties required, and the profaning the day by idleness, or doing that which is in itself sinful, or by unnecessary thoughts, words, or works, about worldly employments or recreations. (Ezekiel 22:26; 23:38; Jer. 17:21; Neh. 13:15,17; Acts 20:7)

Q. 68. What are the reasons annexed to the fourth commandment?
A. The reasons annexed to the fourth commandment are, God's allowing us six days of the week for our own employments, His challenging a special propriety in the seventh, His own example and His blessing the Sabbath day. (Exodus 34:21; 31:16,17; Gen. 2:2,3)

Q. 69. Which is the fifth commandment?
A. The fifth commandment is, "Honor thy father and thy mother, that thy days may be long upon the land which the Lord thy God giveth thee." (Exodus 20:12)

Q. 70. What is required in the fifth commandment?
A. The fifth commandment requires the preserving the honor, and performing the duties, belonging to every one in their several places and relations, as superiors, inferiors, or equals. (Lev. 19:32; 1 Peter 2:17; Rom. 13:1; Eph. 5:21,22; Eph. 6:1,5,9; Col. 3:19-22; Rom. 12:10)

Q. 71. What is forbidden in the fifth commandment?
A. The fifth commandment forbids the neglecting of, or doing anything against the honor and duty which belongs to every one in their several places and relations. (Prov. 30:17; Rom. 13:7,8)

Q. 72. What is the reason annexed to the fifth commandment?
A. The reason annexed to the fifth commandment is a promise of long life and prosperity (as far as it shall serve God's glory and their own good), to all such as keep this commandment. (Eph. 6:2,3; Prov. 4:3-6; 6:20-22)

Q. 73. Which is the sixth commandment?
A. The sixth commandment is, "Thou shalt not kill." (Exodus 20:13)

Q. 74. What is required in the sixth commandment?
A. The sixth commandment requires all lawful endeavors to preserve our own life and the life of others. (Eph. 5:29,30; Ps. 82:3,4; Prov. 24:11,12; Act 16:28)

Q. 75. What is forbidden in the sixth commandment?
A. The sixth commandment forbids the taking away our own life, or the life of our neighbor unjustly, or whatsoever tends thereto. (Gen. 4:10,11; 9:6; Matt. 5:21-26)

Q. 76. Which is the seventh commandment?
A. The seventh commandment is, "Thou shalt not commit adultery."
(Exodus 20:14)

Q. 77. What is required in the seventh commandment?
A. The seventh commandment requires the preservation of our own and our neighbor's chastity, in heart, speech, and behavior. (1 Cor. 6:18; 7:2; 2 Tim. 2:22; Matt. 5:28; 1 Peter 3:2)

Q. 78. What is forbidden in the seventh commandment?
A. The seventh commandment forbids all unchaste thoughts, words, and actions. (Matt. 5:28-32; Job 31:1; Eph. 5:3,4; Rom. 13:13; Col. 4:6)

Q. 79. Which is the eighth commandment?
A. The eighth commandment is, "Thou shalt not steal." (Exodus 20:15)

Q. 80. What is required in the eighth commandment?
A. The eighth commandment requires the lawful procuring and furthering the wealth and outward state of ourselves and others. (Prov. 27:23; Lev. 25:35; Deut. 15:10; 22:1-4)

Q. 81. What is forbidden in the eighth commandment?
A. The eighth commandment forbids whatsoever does or may unjustly hinder our own or our neighbor's wealth or outward state. (1 Tim. 5:8; Prov. 28:19; 23:20,21; Eph. 4:28)

Q. 82. Which is the ninth commandment?
A. The ninth commandment is, "Thou shalt not bear false witness against thy neighbor." (Exodus 20:16)

Q. 83. What is required in the ninth commandment?
A. The ninth commandment requires the maintaining and promoting of truth between man and man, and of our own and our neighbor's good name, especially in witness bearing. (Zech. 8:16; Acts 25:10; Eccles. 7:1; 3 John 12; Prov. 14:5,25)

Q. 84. What is forbidden in the ninth commandment?
A. The ninth commandment forbids whatsoever is pre- judicial to truth, or injurious to our own, or our neighbor's good name. (Eph. 4:25; Ps. 15:3; 2 Cor. 8:20,21)

Q. 85. Which is the tenth commandment?
A. The tenth commandment is, "Thou shalt not covet thy neighbor's house. Thou shalt not covet thy neighbor's wife, nor his man servant, nor his maid servant, nor his ox, nor his ass, nor anything that is thy neighbor's." (Exodus 20:17)

Q. 86. What is required in the tenth commandment?
A. The tenth commandment requires full contentment with our own condition, with a right and charitable frame of spirit towards our neighbor, and all that is his. (Heb. 13:5;1 Tim. 6:6; Rom. 12:15; 1 Cor. 13:4-7; Lev. 19:18)

Q. 87. What is forbidden in the tenth commandment?
A. The tenth commandment forbids all discontentment with our own estate, envying or grieving at the good of our neighbor, and all inordinate motions and affections to anything that is his. (1 Cor. 10:10; James 5:9; Gal. 5:26; Col. 3:5)

Q. 88. Is any man able perfectly to keep the commandments of God?
A. No mere man, since the fall, is able in this life, perfectly to keep the commandments of God, but daily breaks them in thought, word, and deed. (Eccles. 7:20; Gen. 6:5; Gen. 8:21; 1 John 1:8; James 3:8; James 3:2; Rom. 3:23)

Q. 89. What then is the purpose of the law since the fall?

A. The purpose of the law, since, the fall, is to reveal the perfect righteousness of God, that His people may know his will for their lives and the ungodly, being convicted of their sin, may be restrained therein and brought to Christ for salvation. (Ps. 19:7-11; Rom. 3:20,31; 7:7; 12:2; Titus 2:12-14; Gal. 3:22,24; 1 Tim. 1:8)

Q. 90. Are all transgressions of the law equally heinous?

A. Some sins in themselves and by reason of several aggravations, are more heinous in the sight of God than others. (Ezekiel 8:13; John 19:11; 1 John 5:16)

Q. 91. What does every sin deserve?
A. Every sin deserves God's wrath and curse, both in this life, and in that which is to come. (Eph.5:6; Gal. 3:10; Prov. 3:33; Ps. 11:6; Rev. 21:8)

Q. 92. What does God require of us, that we may escape His wrath and curse, due to us for sin?

A. To escape the wrath and curse of God due to us for sin, God requires of us faith in Jesus Christ, repentance unto life, with the diligent use of all the outward and ordinary means whereby Christ communicates to us the benefits of redemption. (Acts 20:21; Acts 16:30,31; 17:30)

Q. 93. What is faith in Jesus Christ?
A. Faith in Jesus Christ is a saving grace, whereby we receive and rest upon Him alone for salvation, as He is offered to us in the Gospel. (Heb. 10:39; John 1:12; Phil. 3:9; Gal. 2:15,16)

Q. 94. What is repentance unto life?

A. Repentance unto life is a saving grace, whereby a sinner, out of a true sense of his sin, and apprehension of the mercy of God in Christ, does, with grief and hatred of his sin, turn from it unto God, with full purpose of, and endeavor after, new obedience. (Acts 2:37; Joel 2:13; Jer. 31:18,19: 2 Cor. 7:10,11; Rom. 6:18)

Q. 95. What are the outward and ordinary means whereby Christ communicates to us the benefits of redemption?
A. The outward and ordinary means whereby Christ communicates to us the benefits of redemption are His ordinances, especially the Word, Baptism, the Lord's Supper and Prayer; all which are made effectual to the elect for salvation. (Rom. 10:17; James 1:18; 1 Cor. 3:5; Acts 14:1; 2:41,42)

Q. 96. How is the Word made effectual to salvation?
A. The Spirit of God makes the reading, but especially the preaching of the Word an effectual means of convincing and converting sinners, and of building them up in holiness and comfort, through faith unto salvation. (Ps. 119:11,18; 1 Thess. 1:6; 1 Peter 2:1,2; Rom. 1:16; Ps. 19:7)

Q. 97. How is the Word to be read and heard that it may become effectual to salvation?

A. That the Word may become effectual to salvation we must attend thereunto with diligence, preparation and prayer, receive it in faith and love, lay it up in our hearts and practice it in our lives. (Prov. 8:34; 1 Peter 2:1,2; 1 Tim. 4:13; Heb. 2:1,3; Heb. 4:2; 2 Thess. 2:10; Ps. 119:11; James 1:21,25)

Q. 98. How do Baptism and the Lord's Supper become effectual means of salvation?

A. Baptism and the Lord's Supper become effectual means of salvation, not from any virtue in them or in him that administers them, but only by the blessing of Christ and the working of His Spirit in them that by faith receive them. (1 Peter 3:21; 1 Cor. 3:6,7; 1 Cor. 12:13)

Q. 99. Wherein do Baptism and the Lord's Supper differ from the other ordinances of God?
A. Baptism and the Lord's Supper differ from the other ordinances of God in that they were specially instituted by Christ to represent and apply to believers the benefits of the new covenant by visible and outward signs. (Matt. 28:19; Acts 22:16; Matt. 26:26-28; Rom. 6:4)

Q. 100. What is Baptism?

A. Baptism is an holy ordinance, wherein the washing with water in the name of the Father, the Son and the Holy Spirit, signifies our ingrafting into Christ and partaking of the benefits of the covenant of grace, and our engagement to be the Lord's. (Matt. 28:19; Rom. 6:3-5; Col. 2:12; Gal. 3:27)

Q. 101. To whom is Baptism to be administered?
A. Baptism is to be administered to all those who actually profess repentance towards God, faith in, and obedience to our Lord Jesus Christ; and to none other. (Acts 2:38; Matt. 3:6; Mark 16:16; Acts 8:12,36; Acts 10:47,48)

Q. 102. Are the infants of such as are professing believers to be baptized?
A. The infants of such as are professing believers are not to be baptized; because there is neither command nor example in the Holy Scriptures, or certain consequence from them, to baptize such.

Q. 103. How is Baptism rightly administered?
A. Baptism is rightly administered by immersion, or dipping the whole body of the person in water, in the name of the Father, and of the Son, and of the Holy Spirit. (Matt. 3:16; John 3:23; Acts 8:38,39)

Q. 104. What is the duty of those who are rightly baptized?
A. It is the duty of those who are rightly baptized to give up (join) themselves to some visible and orderly church of Jesus Christ, that they may walk in all the command- ments and ordinances of the Lord blameless. (Acts 2:46,47; Acts 9:26; 1 Peter 2:5; Heb. 10:25; Rom. 16:5)

Q. 105. What is the visible church?
A. The visible church is the organized society of professing believers, in all ages and places, wherein the Gospel is truly preached and the ordinances of Baptism and the Lord's Supper rightly administered. (Acts 2:42; 20:7; Acts 7:38; Eph. 4:11,12)

Q. 106. What is the invisible church?
A. The invisible church is the whole number of the elect, that have been, are, or shall be gathered into one under Christ the head. (Eph. 1:10; 1:22,23; John 10:16; 11:52)

Q. 107. What is the Lord's Supper?
A. The Lord's Supper is a holy ordinance, wherein, by giving and receiving bread and wine, according to Christ's appointment, His death is showed forth, and the worthy receivers are, not after a corporeal and carnal manner, but by faith, made partakers of His body and blood, with all His benefits, to their spiritual nourishment, and growth in grace. (1 Cor. 11:23-26; 10:16)

Q. 108. What is required to the worthy receiving of the Lord's Supper?
A. It is required of them that would worthily (that is, suitably) partake of the Lord's Supper, that they examine themselves, of their knowledge to discern the Lord's body; of their faith to feed upon Him; of their repentance, love, and new obedience: lest, coming unworthily, they eat and drink judgment to themselves. (1 Cor. 11:27-31; 1 Cor. 5:8; 2 Cor. 13:5)

Q. 109. What is Prayer?

A. Prayer is an offering up of our desires to God, for things agreeable to His will, in the name of Christ, with confession of our sins and thankful acknowledgment of His mercies. (1 John 5:14; 1 John 1:9; Phil. 4:6; Ps. 10:17; 145:19; John 14:13,14)

Q. 110. What rule has God given for our direction in prayer?
A. The whole Word of God is of use to direct us in prayer, but the special rule of direction is that prayer, which Christ taught His disciples, commonly called the Lord's Prayer. (Matt. 6:9-13; 2 Tim. 3:16,17)

Q. 111. What does the preface of the Lord's Prayer teach us?
A. The preface of the Lord's Prayer, which is, "Our Father, which art in heaven," teaches us to draw near to God, with all holy reverence and confidence, as children to a father, able and ready to help us, and that we should pray with and for others. (Matt. 6:9; Luke 11:13; Rom. 8:15; Acts 12:5; 1 Tim. 2:1-3)

Q. 112. What do we pray for in the first petition?

A. In the first petition, which is "Hallowed be thy name," we pray that God would enable us and others to glorify Him in all that whereby He makes Himself known, and that He would dispose all things to His own glory. (Matt. 6:9; Ps. 67:1-3; Rom. 11:36; Rev. 4:11)

Q. 113. What do we pray for in the second petition?

A. In the second petition, which is "Thy kingdom come," we pray that satan's kingdom may be destroyed, and that the kingdom of grace may be advanced; ourselves and others brought into it, and kept in it, and that the kingdom of glory may be hastened. (Matt. 6:10; Ps. 68:1-18; Rom. 10:1; 2 Thess. 3:1; Matt. 9:37,38; Rev. 22:20)

Q. 114. What do we pray for in the third petition?
A. In the third petition, which is, "Thy will be done in earth as it is in heaven," we pray that God by His grace, would make us able and willing to know, obey, and submit to His will in all things, as the angels do in heaven. (Matt. 6:10; Ps. 103:20,21; Ps. 25:4,5; Ps. 119:26)

Q. 115. What do we pray for in the fourth petition?
A. In the fourth petition, which is, "Give us this day our daily bread," we pray that of God's free gift, we may receive a competent portion of the good things of this life and enjoy His blessing with them. (Matt. 6:11; Prov. 30:8,9; 1 Tim. 6:6-8; 4:4,5)

Q. 116. What do we pray for in the fifth petition?
A. In the fifth petition, which is, "And forgive us our debts, as we forgive our debtors," we pray that God, for Christ's sake, would freely pardon all our sins; which we are the rather encouraged to ask, because by His grace we are enabled from the heart to forgive others. (Matt. 6:12; Ps. 51:1,3,7; Mark 11:25; Matt. 18:35)

Q. 117. What do we pray for in the sixth petition?
A. In the sixth petition, which is, "And lead us not into temptation, but deliver us from evil," we pray that God would either keep us from being tempted to sin, or support and deliver us when we are tempted. (Matt. 6:13; 26:41; Ps. 19:13; 1 Cor. 10:13; John 17:15)

Q. 118. What does the conclusion of the Lord's Prayer teach us?
A. The conclusion of the Lord's Prayer, which is, "For thine is the kingdom, and the power, and the glory, forever, Amen," teaches us to take our encouragement in prayer from God only, and in our prayers to praise Him, ascribing kingdom, power, and glory to Him; and in testimony of our desire, and assurance to be heard, we say, AMEN. (Matt. 6:13; Dan. 9:18,19; 1 Chron. 29:11-13; 1 Cor. 14:16; Phil. 4:6; Rev. 22:20)

Made in United States
Orlando, FL
01 November 2022

24111241R00065